# 7 Techniques of Healing

## How I Overcame Abuse to Live My Authentic Life

ERICA LYNN

Copyright © 2018 by Erica Lynn.
All rights reserved. No part of this publication may be reproduced, distributed, or transmitted in any form or by any means, including photocopying, recording, or other electronic or mechanical methods, without the prior written permission of the publisher, except in the case of brief quotations embodied in critical reviews and certain other noncommercial uses permitted by copyright law.

www.1stepbeyondu.com

ISBN 13: 978-1-7274-6883-0

Printed in the United States of America

# ACKNOWLEDGEMENTS

Thanks to all my friends and family for all the love and support;
To my mom, Martha, for the unconditional love;
To the loving memory of my dad,
Willie Sr, you would have been so proud of me;
To Novah, my best friend since the sixth grade, for always standing up for me;
To my sisters and brother, Dawn, Darlene, and Willie Jr.;
To my pastor, Leon McDonald III;
To my children, Q'lante, Deja, and Jalen,
I reserve special thanks to my mentor; for the wonderful impact you made in my life.
Listening to me cry through countless nights when I was down and lacked vision. Thank you for fighting for me when I couldn't find the strength to do so myself. Thank you for your selflessness and sheer determination to help me arrive at my point of purpose.

# CONTENTS

1. HEAL ........................................................................................... 9
2. EDUCATE ................................................................................. 22
3. ACTION .................................................................................... 32
4. LEAP ........................................................................................ 41
5. INSPIRE ................................................................................... 50
6. NEED ....................................................................................... 60
7. GROWTH ................................................................................. 66

# 7 TECHNIQUES of HEALING

## How I Overcame Abuse to Live My Authentic Life

### ERICA LYNN

# CHAPTER 1

## HEAL

As we begin our journey in the discovery of healing together, there will be moments along the way where you will be required to stop and re-evaluate your life. Moments like these may give rise to you asking yourself introspective questions like, "Why did I make that choice?" or "Why did I go down that road?" You will soon discover the reasons why as you go along in this book. Many women go through life beating themselves up because they were not the super mom, or the super wife, or the super boss, they set out to be. If you, like them, continue to fault yourself for every mistake you've made, then your healing process can very well be delayed.

**The core essence of healing is for you to identify and become the best version of yourself.**

Becoming the best version of you could mean starting your business, becoming a parent for the first time or second time, helping others, being a great spouse, or becoming a pastor. These are just a few examples to consider. It is pertinent that you not have to choose between your home life and your work life, but instead find a balance.

It has often been said that healing comes from within in the pursuit of balance. Finding balance is within. It is within the deep parts of your body, mind, and soul which more often than not is the difference between breakthrough and disappointment. As we get started on this journey of healing, I would like to open with an exercise to help clear your thoughts and allow the process to begin:

1: **Close your eyes**. As you close your eyes I want you to think back to that one experience that caused you pain or caused you to hold back. Now, think about all the details around that story. What happened leading up to the event? What happened during and after the event?

2. **Inhale and Exhale**. Inhale deeply and as you do so, count to five. Exhale on that same five counts. Repeat the inhale and exhale on a five count step, but this time, as you exhale, say to yourself, "I forgive myself" or "I forgive the other person." Whoever or what it is, in order to receive, releasing is a must. Now, open your eyes. This step is the most important step in the healing process because often times in life, we cannot move forward into

our futures because we are stuck in our past. If I hadn't gone through this last step myself, I would not be the author of the 7 Techniques of healing.

I remember coming home from school one day only to find out my father had left and he was not coming back. I wasn't afforded the privilege of the "your dad and I are separating conversation"; instead, I just came home and he was gone. I was devastated, and as a result, I became what my family would later label a "wild child". No one could handle or control me. I developed what I call the "daddy syndrome," looking for love in all the wrong places.

*I believe that men and women can cause their children to be in pursuit of the love that was not giving to them by their parents.*

This possibly may affect a large part of the population. However, that was the beginning of a long arduous road that I was about to begin. I often share stories of the things I've gone through because I find it necessary, and in order to bring healing and greatness out in others. So, I must share what is inside of me as well as the healing I received. Your past cannot define your future. Instead, it can only bring an understanding to the person you are about to become. This book is broken down into acronyms, with each chapter denoting a part of the word 'HEALING'.

H-Heal, E-Educate, A-Action, L-Leap, I-Inspire, N-Need, and G-Growth. These will be the steps that will propel you into the next level of your life.

As I was faced with my healing process, I realized that my past totally controlled the woman that I was. After my father left, I began to live a life of self-destruction, drinking, smoking, and partying. My mother could barely control or had the time for me because she had issues of her own that she needed healing from. At the age of sixteen, I was diagnosed with migraine episodes. When I turned 19, I went to college.

I remember the final day of exam. I got up very early and dressed up, ready to enjoy the beautiful day. So, I grabbed my bag and went down the stairwell to the front door and as soon as I opened the door, the sunlight came piercing my eyes directly. Immediately, I shut the door, went back upstairs and got into bed. It was the start of an episode. As usual, it started with sensitivity to light, then spots would dance across my eyes, followed by a loss of vision and excruciating pain.

I would become nauseous and vomit for intermittently

for four to six hours. My body would often go cold and then hot, drastically. These episodes usually weakened me to the extent where I would pass out on the bathroom floor. Sometimes, I'd be on the bathroom floor until a member of the family came around and put me in bed where I'd be, for one to two days, watching my whole life flash past me. The migraine cost me a great deal, one of which was my inability to complete college, because my professor refused to accept acute episodic migraine as an excusable diagnosis back then. The migraines certainly changed my perspective and caused me to look at life differently.

## *I would often be overwhelmed with thoughts that I didn't have a chance in life to advance.*

As a reaction to those thoughts, I felt if that I got a man, he would be there for me and love me —that, he would never hurt me. This was to be the early steps in a tortuous journey that had me finding love in all the wrong places. Party after party, relationship after relationship, I was left stranded in the hope that Mr. Right was out there somewhere. What I discovered was, if you ask for trouble, then trouble is what you get.

At the age of seventeen, I decided to become a female dancer. I figured surely, I will find Mr. Right. I remember going to a club on the west side of Detroit for my audition to the great life, or so I thought. As I went up on stage and danced, I will never forget the feeling. It was the feeling that I'd lowered myself to a person my parents would not be proud of. Of course, I found solace in the thought that this surely couldn't be all life had to offer me.

On the one hand, I had always dreamt of one day becoming an actor or standing on stage in front of large crowds, turning heads. On the other hand, I had no idea that dancing in a club would be it. When I finished my dance, the DJ came and through a pile of money taken from the stage and that changed my perspective instantly.

However, I shortly discovered that I was underage and did not have the proper licensing to be in the club, so I had to go underground and do private parties. I would never wish experiences like this for other young women. It is one of the least desirable paths a young woman can tread because it can possibly mean life or death to some, and a loss of the inner-self to others. I was on the precipice and inches away from death and irredeemable addiction to drugs.

A part of me felt the violation I was subjecting my body to, while the other side of me was simply having fun.

Eventually, it all came to an end when I saw the repercussions of my actions in how it really hurt a very close family member. The disappointment in her eyes spoke more than a thousand words. I knew that I'd let her down. I left the dancing industry after about six months.

**After my short career as a stripper, I went on to meet a man who was seven years my senior and we began a short dating process.**

At the time, my mom and I were staying at my sister's one-bedroom apartment, sleeping on her couch. I knew that although my sister had a great job working in the hospital, she could not care financially for her two little kids, my mom and myself. So, when I met this man, the process moved pretty fast as my options were minimal. I was all but packaged up with decorative ribbons and handed to him so to speak.

Because I was so wild, my mom encouraged the relationship as she felt that it would slow my pace. It was in the course of this relationship that I became pregnant with the first of my three kids. All that I could remember, at the time, was that my father had left and I did not want my child or children to grow up without one. This marked the start of allowing my past to dictate the level of abuse that was to come. I'm not saying that it was a knock-out, drop-down, drag-out or world war II level of abuse, but the level of verbal abuse that I experienced in this ten-year span took a toll on me and a long time to heal from. In writing this book, I found it to be of utmost importance to have an understanding of the root problem.

The process of healing may result in you going at it all alone. If that is so, I would advise that you seek out help. The bible says strength is in numbers. Ecclesiastes 4:9-10, *"Two are better than one, because they have a good return for their labor: If either of them falls down, one can help the other up. But pity anyone who falls and has no one to help them up."* Do not fight through your demons alone. Note that the help you seek will vary from person to person. From my experience, I needed a whole lot of people to help me. I reached out to my pastor, friends, I hired a coach, and most importantly, I sought God. Matthew 6:33 "*But seek first his kingdom and his righteousness, and all these things will be given to you as well."* I had to be willing to go in with my eyes, heart, and soul open and a willingness to do the work that was required.

If you are not ready to do the work, this may result in you getting the same results that you have always received. Imagine for a second that your problem was that you drank too much; while others classified you as an alcoholic, you classified yourself as a social drinker. Then you begin having a drink every day and if something happened in your life, you turned to alcohol as an escape.

As events take place, your alcohol consumption goes over the top. Every time, you would drink, afterwards, you would wake up and discover a total stranger next to you on the bed. Eventually, you find yourself waking up and asking what happened the last night or calling people to apologize for what you did last night. That, for every problem, is the indication that it is time to call a spade a spade and step into your healing. It is time to put the steps into action.

## *In order to take action, you must start within yourself.*

I can always help by equipping you with the necessary tools. I may even attend meetings with you but it would mean nothing if you are not ready to do what is required. Luke 12:48 *"But the one who does not know and does things deserving punishment will be beaten with few blows. From everyone who has been given much, much will be demanded; and from the one who has been entrusted with much, much more will be asked."* In my translation, to whom much is given much is required. In order for God to bless you or help you through a situation, you must be willing to do the work.

In order to heal, first identify the problem. This can vary from person to person. One person could be very self-aware and know what the problem already is but does not have the strength or the courage to do the work. Whereas, another person might need help identifying the problem. However, the most important key is having the willingness to be transparent enough in order to do what is necessary. That means if you need a therapist or counselor to help, then you have to go to a therapist or counselor. When seeking a mentor or a friend whom you trust and love, do not allow them to be your only options. Perhaps, attend (AA) alcohol anonymous, (NA) narcotics anonymous, or (SA) Sexual addiction.

As you go through this process, it is necessary to be for you to be open, to listen, and to accept constructive criticism about yourself. Looking closely will be massively advantageous in helping you identify the problem.

I will give you an example. One of my problems was that I always looked for love from men (notice I said one of my problems to indicate that I knew I had more than one). I felt that, if they loved me it would hold me and keep me secure and I would be happy and I would live happily ever after. What I discovered is that I wanted love so bad, I ended up looking for it in all the wrong places. I ignored all the signs that were originally there just so that I could have a good-looking man on my arm, who would treat me like a queen.

I discovered in the process that, had I done the work, I would have been able to identify when all a man tells me, "you're beautiful and if you give me what I want, then I will give you what you want."

**Any woman who knows her self-worth and value, would have responded to such a man by telling him, "I am not willing to compromise my values or integrity because you think I should."**

Now, I say this because my father came back into my life, strongly, for the last three years of his life. And I received a level of love, strength, and healing that I had never seen, heard, or felt before. After my father returned, he suffered a heart attack in 2014. This was the first of nine attacks he would experience over a three year period. Each time he had an attack, his heart would flatline completely (only to be brought back by the defibrillator that was installed after his first attack) and he would end up in the hospital

It was after one of such attacks that I went to the hospital two days later, he looked like he was recovering. He was sitting up on his bed, laughing and talking. Then I remember telling him, "Daddy, I want a divorce." He paused and said, "Well Erica, why do you want a divorce? When you guys were here together two days ago you looked so happy." I told him, "That was a front. I had put him out a week ago, then you became ill and I did not want to disappoint you, knowing that we have not been married for a year."

The powerful part of this work was that after explaining to my dad that I made a mistake by wanting love and did not take the time to really get to know him. That I did not take the time to really know if he was angry or verbally and physically abusive to women. That I knew I repeated the same cycle of being with a man because I needed the financial support.

The powerful part of this confession was that it resulted in my father and I having a very intense and defining conversation in that hospital room in 2014.

I had the divorce papers in my purse and I signed them. What came afterwards, for the next three years was that my father loved me, he poured into me which helped me develop the ability to discern what real love is. Sadly, my father passed on in 2017, but I will never forget that conversation with him.

A way to remember and identify what you take away from this chapter is to write it down. As you conclude this chapter, it will be necessary for you to look at where you're coming from in order to understand where you are going. I do not want you to think for a moment that you're done with healing after one breakthrough. There is a lot of work to be done. And it all begins with the past because it is a fundamental step toward completing the next six steps in the process.

# CHAPTER 2

# EDUCATE / EMPOWER

Imagine that your life was a topsy-turvy battle and you were trying to figure out how to stabilize everything happening to you. Then you question, "How do I make this happen?" This is what chapter two is about; asking yourself deep questions and seeking out the answer. This can be used not only to help yourself but also to help educate and empower others. For me, these questions were, "Why did an older man, who was a neighbor, decided to touch me in inappropriate places and I did nothing about it at the age of thirteen?" "Why did God allow me to go through the struggles in my mind for over twenty years?" "What is it about me that warrants people to protect me but yet others want to do harm to me?"

Getting answers to these questions meant that I had to understand what happened, and in order to do so, I had to reach out and ask for help. How can I help others, if I do not understand what truly took place or even know how to articulate it in words? In life, situations happen where we are not able to move forward due to a lack of knowledge. I remember going to see my second therapist/counselor in my early thirties. I had just come out of a ten-year abusive marriage and I jumped into another relationship thinking that this would be better. I remember telling the therapist (of my relationship) that we would only spend time together late in the evenings. This was partly because I had to work and also had to take care of my children during the day so the only free time I had were late evenings.

And when he had an off day, he did not want to spend time with me during the day. I remember being so frustrated, sad, and disappointed (I still have my journal entries from that period). However, I never expressed my true feelings to him because it was his way and no other way. I did not have the backbone to stand up to him and really push that my needs were not being met, instead, I suppressed all my wants and desires.

## *I accepted what was given to me. I would shut down, not communicate, and instead stay silent.*

Yet, on the inside, I was boiling red. From the outside looking in, it seemed easy to stand up to and express how I felt to him. But, in hindsight, the intense level of verbal abuse I suffered at the hands of my first husband had broken me down to my core. And there were days where I only manage to hang on to my sanity by a thin strand.

Instead of effective communication, I simply stepped out and cheated on him for a whole summer, traveling around from state to state with one individual I worked with. Yes, that is correct; from the perspective of an outsider, I did not handle the situation properly.

Despite seeing a therapist, I discovered my self-esteem to be so low along with the need to learn how to handle situations by not keeping them bottled up inside. When you bottle things up, it may trigger results that you cannot take back. I realized that when people saw me, their first thought was, "there's a beautiful woman with three children, who'd light up any room she walks into if only she had a clue about the powers she possessed."

When you become educated about the things in your life, you become powerful and unstoppable. When a person goes to college, they enter a little unsure of who they are or the career they want to pursue. In the end, the result of them attending college is a complete life change, so much so that they are not the way they were when they first went in. They end up having read more books and become more knowledgeable about their course of study. Also, the level of confidence gained during the whole college experience will allow them to not only receive their degree, but set higher standards as well. These standards can be geared toward their career choices, relationships, and friendships that will take place in the future.

***On this journey of self-discovery, you will learn a lot about yourself and when you're able to stand in your truth, own it and move on, then you would have reached another level.***

However, we have to continue to do more work to get there. If I had stayed in counseling and actually did the work that was required, I probably would have been a lot further off in life than I am now. In order to heal, that meant I needed to reveal what happened to me, to my mother. I was sixteen years old waking up in the middle of the night from terrifying nightmares, cold sweats, and panic attacks. My mom did not understand where my anger and rage were coming from. I was so disrespectful, wouldn't listen to anyone.

I had to finally tell my mom what happened. I just remember that at age thirteen, I was often asked to go help clean my neighbor's house in order to earn extra money. Whenever I went to his house, I would most times wear a big coat in the middle of summer. This was because he was always asking for a hug before giving me the money or item I was asked to go and get. It started with just a simple hug. Progressively, due to his arms being so long while hugging me, his arms would go completely around my body to my breast. Every time he hugged me, he'd squeeze my breast. I thought if I wore a big coat that I could not feel it whenever he touched me. However, that did not work because he would just unzip my jacket, resulting into more skin contact.

I remember being asked to have him take me to the store one day to get a few items for dinner. That turned out to be the longest ride of my life — it certainly felt like it. After completing the grocery shopping, I attempted to sit in the back but he was very adamant about me sitting in the front. I agreed and sat as close to the door as I could, staring out through the window. He gently grabbed me and pulled me closer to him.

Back then, cars did not have the middle consul that they have today. He put the car in drive and as he drove, the touching started. He began touching me all over my body from top to bottom. Wherever his hands could fit while he drove, he would put them there. I remember trying to squeeze my body together as tightly as I could, thinking that it would not let him reach certain places, however, he was very strong. I never told anyone what happened, or why I was out of control, because at that time, I did not know or understand. I was already on the fast track of life but did not know where I was going or how I was going to get there. What I did know was that the pent-up emotions and feelings would eventually have to come out, I just wasn't sure how.

### *The road to discovery is the road you seek. Do not stop when the lesson gets hard and you feel like balling up, shutting down and crying.*

It is ok to cry but, do not let your tears consume you and stop you from your lesson. Avoid living in your tears; live past them. I think that is such a powerful statement because all too often, we let fear stop us, we let fear dictate to us that we cannot go forth and be one of God's greatest creation.

I want you to write down three situations or things that have held you back. These situations or things have most likely held you back in life and are what you need healing from. It could be something obstructing your pathway to the next level in your career. It could be a family situation that you cannot dust off your shoulder. Whatever it is, write it down.

1._____

2._____

3._____

This is your first step towards education and empowerment. You have made an agreement with yourself that it is time to let go of what is stopping you and lay it in God's hands. In order to achieve this, I want to start with a little exercise that you can use whenever you're feeling stressed or overwhelmed.

**Recite the following:**

> *I am leaving these matters of (include what you wrote on lines 1, 2, 3) in God's hands.*
>
> *I will no longer walk around with them on my shoulder but instead walk in my purpose, and what I am designed to do.*

Now I want you to close your eyes and take a deep breath, count 1,2,3 and breathe out. And as you do so, release everything that has held you back. Next, repeat this process at least three (3) times until you feel it in your heart and soul. If you are like me, and feel a little bit teary, go ahead and grab a tissue and wipe away all the tears of release. After you do this exercise take a look at yourself in the mirror and know that you are the best creation that God has made.

**This step that you have done was and is the biggest education that you will ever get because now that you know what has held you back, it is time to move forward.**

Life is like an airplane ride, the stewardess welcomes and tells you where your seat is. Before you take your seat, you put your bag up top in the luggage compartment. The stewardess comes around and tells you to buckle up, and the sign says, "please fasten your seat belt." You settle down and make yourself comfortable. The seat belt and no smoking signs ding on. You begin to approach the runway; the stewardess goes through the things you need to know ahead of time, in case of an emergency.

If you're lucky, you may end up with a funny stewardess who makes you laugh and forget this could be a smooth ride or the ride of a lifetime. The plane takes off, everything is going well and you should be at your destination in two hours. All of a sudden, there is a turbulence, it startles you a little but stops quickly. Then out of nowhere, the pilot's voice comes on through the system and says, "We have experienced multiple engine failure and we are going down ladies and gentlemen, please put your seatbelts on and brace yourself for impact."

As the plane is spiraling down you are praying, asking God for forgiveness, wishing you had told your loved ones you love them. You start to wish that you'd spent more time with the kids and husband. "I should have forgiven myself for what happened to me as a child because it was not my fault." All of these go through your mind in a flash. The level of fear makes you yell out, "oh God please help me! I will go back and fix it, I will fix myself, I will stop living in my past. God, I know people are depending on me." You start making deals with God, then all of a sudden you feel a difference in the cabin pressure and you hear the pilot say, "ladies and gentlemen we have regained full use of the engines and everything will be ok. We will prepare for an emergency landing to switch planes." The plane stabilizes and soon lands. Then as you exit the plane, you know it and can feel it that your life will never be the same again. You know that you must fix the brokenness that is within you in order to move forward and heal.

In the same vein as one who had an epiphany on an eventful plane ride, It is time for you to take action. It is time to move forward and work on your new life. I am already excited to read all the wonderful testimony-filled emails I'll be receiving as a result of the healing that will take place in your life from through this book.

# CHAPTER 3

# ACTION

All too often, the picture of what needs to be done is painted right in front of us. However, the way to get there is not so clear. If you're starting a new business and you have completed the basic steps —such as registering the business, getting a tax EIN number, and developing the business' core concept— the next step is to take action. You must do the work that is essential to the prosperity of the business e.g. target market survey, target market demographic analysis, target market consumer behavior analysis etc.

These steps will help you in your developmental phase. Expecting someone else to do the work for you is not going through the process. Get your hands dirty and do the work yourself. This is the one sure way you can understand the mechanics and details of your business. In order to achieve the goal, you have set for yourself, "you must be willing to work as hard as you breathe" (often said by Eric Thomas) or else, your business or idea will stop. This is the approach you must take when it comes to all aspects of your life. If healing is what you want, then you must be willing to work hard for it.

I would often dream of having a successful business traveling all over the world. Having business relationship with men and women and having a level of respect from them. As you have read earlier, I had a rough start figuring things out. I do not want to give you the impression that things went south with every person I met. What I will say is that not having the level of understanding of how to control my flirt mostly worked against me.

## *When I decided to change the reality of how my past affected my future, I had to take action.*

The first step I took was to go to God. I prayed about it, I said the words audibly — about what my past experiences were and how they affected me. I began speaking to my pastor, ensuring that I was totally transparent even though I did not know if I would be judged or what the outcome would be. I received some great advice and counsel. One of the things my pastor told me was to create an ending for my book.

For the next two years, I spent time on personal development, working hard on myself and self-analyzing. I asked myself what it is that I must do, knowing that writing an ending will be an ongoing process that I can document as I go through it all? I remember watching Lisa Nichols one day and she told a powerful story of how she needed to buy diapers for her baby but only had $12 dollars and some change in the bank while being on public assistance. How she went through the next couple of days wrapping her baby in towels because she could not afford diapers. How she felt broke and broken.

Also, she went on to talk about writing checks — "funding my dreams"— that she sent to a savings account she never touched. One day, she went to the bank and discovered she had fifty something thousand dollars saved up. Her perseverance paid off because this money was used to start her business.

I remember weeping while listening to her share the story of the time she told her son, "they will never be broke again." After hearing her story, I cried for days trying to figure out why my life was such a mess. Guess what? I took action and at the age of forty, I began to start my life over. You too must be willing to start life over. Being willing to change and take the necessary action.

Walking in alignment with your purpose is a big part of taking action. I will explain. Have you ever met someone that says they want to lose fifty or one hundred pounds? But, every day, you see them smoking, partying, drinking, and catching the munchies in the mental daze of life. This person lacks self-control, using the kids as an excuse to cook unhealthy fatty foods. They barely exercise since working out and getting high at the same time don't quite mix. And people would often remind this person of the enormous potential they have and that they have to realize it for themselves.

**That person was me until I began to take action in my life and change all the things that had been holding me back for years which quite frankly was myself.**

I could not do what some people do and still have a drink occasionally or smoke occasionally, I had to quit everything. I went cold turkey all at once. Of course, I prayed about it and would always ask for strength. If anyone knew me then and often prayed for me or with me, my one request would be that they pray for me to have strength. At the time, I never knew that I was asking God for the strength to do all the things that I am doing now and all the things he was about to reveal to me.

What I did know was that in order to lose the weight, I needed to change. I had to stop doing and walk away from the things that continually ensured that I stagnated. I had to stop living my life on both sides of the fence. I opened the gate and walked out completely through it while slamming it shut behind me. If I ever get confused and want to quit and go back, all I have to do is turn around and look over the fence to remind myself where I came from, remind myself that I am no longer living on that side of the fence any longer.

You might think the above was a story about me losing weight. No, not in the literal sense. It was me finding it difficult to commit myself fully to anything without committing myself to GOD first. I had to walk into God's purpose for me.

I'd like us to go back to the most important chapter so far, "healing". Healing is an action, in order to heal, starting from the inside is important because your outside can be just a mask. Although you may start a successful business, relationship, weight loss journey or becoming a mom, eventually, your inside will burst out and may cause you to lose it all. Have you ever met a person who self-sabotages? This person automatically thinks the outcome is going to be bad so before the bad thing happens, they ruin it or quit before the real ending happens. I'm sure some of you or someone you know will be able to relate with this. Such a person is afraid of going after that big business deal because they feel their proposal will be turned down, so they don't even try. This person will never accept my idea, they will never want to do business with me. And one I was particularly prone to: Allowing someone who might be out of my pay grade or league to love me. Feeling inferior or inadequate because someone else is smarter or more successful than you are while you're still trying to figure out your life.

Truth be told, everyone's still trying to figure out things in their lives. This and much more, it is time to take action by working on yourself. Open the door and allow love to come in and find you.

## *Do not run at the first sign of adversity. If you want good results then take good action.*

Action is more than doing, it can also be a feeling or a thought process. Falling victim to inaction is what happens to people when they tell themselves 'I cannot', or 'I am afraid'. I know that there are a lot of different individual experience out there and I can't possibly touch on and break down each one. That is why I implore and encourage you to break down your own situation by taking action. I knew a lady who was sexually abused as a child.

She was always angry and out of control, emotional and mean. She was promiscuous and would curse you out on sight. People often thought that she was extra since her personality was very noticeable. She was loved by everyone because she was always the life of the party and could cook her butt off. When she was in her happy place, she would often make people laugh and brighten their day.

The one thing about her was that she had so much love to give, but she did not know how to give love without looking for something in return. That was part of her make up. It resulted in her inability to stay in a marriage or even cope generally, sometimes. While being a mother and a grandmother would often keep her going, every time she tried to move ahead in life, the things in her head would get to her and she would have nervous breakdowns. Her children had to grow up pretty fast.

Being a divorcée single mom meant there were times when she just could not handle it all. But still, she'd manage to hold on by the skin of her teeth. After running most of her life from one man to another; one situation to another; one state to another, she got tired. She could not run anymore. She decided to take it to God. She decided to go to therapy and get help for the sexual abuse. She even had an opportunity to tell her abuser what he had done even though he was much older by this time. This freed her and allowed her to move on with her life, and let go of the hurt and pain that was inside her. It allowed her to understand what love really was to her. And it all happened because she took action and received help in fixing her inside. Although this woman is up in age now and never found her true love, she is sharing her story because she knows that there are a lot of people with similar experience who might find her breakthrough to be the inspiration they need.

## Getting help is imperative. Do not hold it in.

I know this goes for both men and women, the one thing I have learned in my training on domestic violence and abuse program is that men and women alike suffer from abuse. During my research, I came across a National crime victimization survey about rape and sexual violence of 40,000 households in America. The statistics showed that 38% of men had experienced sexual abuse or some form of sexual molestation incident against them. When I talk about sexual abuse, I draw on real-life stories and experiences that have happened to real people.

Now is the time to take action, write down the steps you have learned and use them to your benefit. This will not only help you heal but also allow you to move forward in your life and be a blessing to others.

1._____

2._____

3._____

When I say take action, I mean take action. If weight loss is what you want, change your diet and exercise. If starting a business is what you want, write down the core outline of your business and the name of your company, get off the couch and go register your business' name — it will only cost you $10. This will help get your wheels spinning. Healing yourself, forgiving yourself, and attaining self-love again, will require you to start today, right now…so, don't wait. Dust your past off your shoulders, and walk up right into your new life. Take action and I guarantee that you are about to take the biggest LEAP you have ever taken in your life.

# CHAPTER 4

## LEAP

I remember waking up the next day after I made the decision to start my own business and feeling such a vibrant rush from knowing that I will never work for someone else, ever again. The reality of living a life of fear was gone, never to return. In this chapter, we are going to discuss how you can take a leap into your best life. Here, you will learn what you need to do, elevate yourself, gain access to all the things you will need, and tap into your full potential. Learn, Elevate, Access, Potential, L.E.A.P. This method will help you if you get confused and are not sure about what to do next, as you take your leap.

We have kicked life in the butt and it is time to make powerful affirmations like,

I am **powerful**.
I am **beautiful**.
I am **wonderfully made**.
I am **healed**.
I am **successful**.
I am **a great mother**.
I am **the best person for the job**.
I am **ready for that promotion**.
I am **a great chef**.
I am **a superb CEO**.

The power of 'I am' will tap into a place in your mind, causing a paradigm shift. Philippians 4:13 says, *I can do all things through Christ who strengthens me.* What I would like you to do is, get some index cards and put them all around your house. Put them in places that you frequently go to and can read them on a daily basis.

I want you to write each of the following on each card:

*I am powerful*

*I am beautiful*

*I am fantastically, graciously, and wonderfully made*

*I am worth it*

*I am somebody*

These next two are my favorites and I came across them from listening to the great Les Brown.

*I must be willing to do the things today, in order to have the things tomorrow, that others won't have.*

*Good things are supposed to happen to me.*

The next one is credited to Ms. Lisa Nichols

*I will never be broke again.*

As you write these on different index cards, placing them strategically through your home, you will begin to attract the positivity, therein, that you have put out in the atmosphere. If you're unsure about the places to put the cards, you may choose to follow my example. I have mine in the bathroom on the mirror; on the side of the wall as I'm putting my make up on. This might be a little (TMI) too much information, but I also have one on the side of the commode that I can read in the mornings when I get up.

## Place these cards wherever you can. Make sure to repeat them ten times a day.

If you do this for thirty days straight, you will start to see a shift — even after the fifth day. The level of change that will start to take place in your life and in your thoughts will be phenomenal. Learning what is needed to keep your spirits going as you are taking the leap is very important.

Now, this will help you understand how to elevate yourself into your higher purpose. Let's imagine for a second that you wanted to get to the top floor of the office building, this is where all the magic happens. The biggest deals are made there. You have seen people go to the top floor; they go in one way and come out successful millionaires. You say to yourself, "wow I wish I could go to the top floor and come out a millionaire. What do they have that I do not have?" You start to think, then you begin asking all the right questions. "It's not what do they have but what do I have? What can I take to the top floor and come out a millionaire?"

This is the point at which you begin to research the prerequisites for making it to the top floor. Every day, you work on your idea or your business or yourself and as you learn, you start doing what is needed. Then one day, you get a personal invitation to the top floor. You're shaking in your boots wondering what is about to happen. You go in, and as you walk through those doors, you see where all the magic happens, a sense of calmness comes over you.

Your head is held high, your confidence is on level ten and you go through with your pitch and the deal happens. Everything goes better than you expected. Well, ladies and gentlemen, this all happened because you elevated your thinking and took a leap of faith. You took a leap in believing in yourself, that you can access whatever you put your mind to. You did the work without clamming up and running off. This elevation happens when you have told yourself that you can do it. In this example, you wanted to rise to the top floor but you had to figure out how to get there first.

**Sometimes, taking that leap is the only way to get there. Do not let anything stop you or get in your way.**

I would be lying if I told you there would be no sacrifices. The truth is, in order to get to where you are going, you have to be ready and in order to get there, you have to start with your mind.

Steve Harvey did a talk about jump where he said, "sometimes, when you jump, the parachute might not open." There are going to be many reasons why you tell yourself not to jump. There will be many excuses. Some will possibly be great excuses and reasons to hold you back. Whatsoever the excuses are, eventually when you jump, I promise you that the parachute will eventually open and you will land into your purpose.

This all happened because you leaped, you believed that all things are possible. Do not be afraid. Have faith. Have faith in your purpose, have faith in the divine plan, have faith that your dreams and visions will come true. Remember the old saying that, "nothing comes to a sleeper but a dream." It is one thing to have the dream but it is another thing to act on your dream. As you take action into what you see, always remember that your vision is your vision.

Other people may not see the vision as clearly as you do. Do not allow the fact that they cannot see what you see, the way you see it, to stop you. One day, you will look up and time will have passed you by. Les Brown said, "The graveyard is the richest place on earth, because it is here that you will find all the hopes and dreams that were never fulfilled, the books that were never written, the songs that were never sung, the inventions that were never shared, the cures that were never discovered, all because someone was too afraid to take the first step, keep up with the problem, or determined to carry out their dream."

You see, there were millions of people with wonderful ideas that they never shared; ideas that were never birthed because, instead of taking a leap into greatness, they took a leap the other way round. In other the words, they took these ideas and dreams to their graves.

Do not wake up one day just to realize that your time has passed you by, and that one person you could have inspired to reach their full potential, did not reach it. I encourage you to leap. I implore you to rise up and show the world who you really are. "What am I leaping into?" You might be asking this question right now. You are leaping into your greatness.

## *You have so much to offer the world.*

Technology has made life so much easier these days. Supposing you are a stay-at-home mom, who cannot work outside the home due to childcare issues for example. Then you have a great idea like an in-home daycare; online business; virtual assistant; secret shopper; author, etc. that will help your life become easier with the housework. Now that you have an idea of what you want to do, start researching and finding out what you need to start, create, or invent your idea.

Self-knowledge/education is the key to an abundant and prosperous life. One of the number one online resources you can take advantage of is Google. If you have the internet, you can research and find out just about anything. When I was growing up, Encyclopedia Britannica and the library were the only self-education sources for me. Now, there are so many tools and techniques you can utilize to help you obtain the knowledge. Once you get started with your research, begin the development stage. It might not be totally clear to you at this point, but if you have done the work and Googled the hottest trends and discovered that there is a need for your product or service, then you are headed in the right direction. You see how easy that was? At this point you have:

1. Come up with an idea
2. Done your research
3. Had an understanding of what the hottest trends are
4. Learned about your market

Now, you must begin to develop and nurture your idea. It is like a flower, you must water it and take care of it. Give it sunlight, talk to your plant. Give it life. You should know that the moment you stop nurturing your flower, the leaves will begin to wilt away.

As soon as you add water and sunlight it will sprout right back up. Don't allow your ideas in life to become a wilted flower, keep watering and nurturing your idea until it becomes what you want it to become. If you look back and think about the things you have walked away from in order to arrive at this point of healing, you will realize that these circumstances moved and allowed you to think about how to put the pieces of your life together. This was done in order to consider starting a business, applying for a new job, going after that promotion, losing weight, finding love, while being present with your family.

## *Always remember that success is what you make out of it.*

What you put in is what you get out. Do not allow someone else to define what your success is or should be. Instead, go forward and take the leap into your visualized greatness. When you see the dream or vision, make sure it is big, make sure the aim is high and imagine all possibilities. One day, you're going to look up and discover that the leap you took, God had a plan for it. Do not walk, leap into your greatness.

# Chapter 5

## INSPIRE

In writing this book I have had the opportunity of discovering a lot about myself. Living my normal, everyday life of greatness has helped me walk into my purpose. On the road to discovery while building my vision and dreams, I identified that I have very specific standards. The question might arise, why is that not a given? Going back to the talk I had with my pastor, I said to him "as I am changing and discovering who I am, the one thing that I aspire to have is business relationships with men and have them respect me as a person and business colleague. I want to stop walking around with a sign on my forehead saying she has a past."

What I learned as I began to go through the changes is, people will only do what you allow them to do. If I allow men to treat me any other way than a woman of God, a Queen, and a respected pillar of the community, then that is what they will do. The "#Metoo" movement gained a lot of traction and has been seismic. This is a time where awareness about unruly behaviors that took place between men and women in the past are brought to the light. This is a time when women can set their standards and get respect in return. Integrity is something that we all must have.

I knew at one point in my life that I did not have any morals and values when I started having children at eighteen. I was young and did not have a clue. I knew how to cook and clean and work, but had no real values to pass on to my son at that age. Married at the age of nineteen, the only concern of value I had was, not wanting my children to be born out of wedlock.

I was insistent on only having my children by one man. Please know that I hold no prejudice or disrespect toward those who do have more than one father (or baby daddy) for their children. My feelings are as strong as they are because everyone was telling me I was too young. Someone also told me that, "I would end up as a statistic, and I would never amount to anything if I started having children at such an early age." I was determined to prove everyone wrong, I was serious about being a great mother regardless of the circumstances.

I learned that you can always change directions at any time. As I went through my ten-year marriage of verbal and mental abuse. I stayed in it because I did not want to be a statistic; I was determined to be more than that.

**_If anyone looked deeper then, they'd see how affected I was by my father leaving at such a young age and know that I did not want any of that for my children._**

To me, I was standing my ground and staying true to my word that I would be missing the bigger picture of honest and strong morals values. In hindsight, what I was teaching my kids was that it is ok to be in a relationship with a man that treats and talks to you disrespectfully as he so pleases. Perhaps, you are also in a place right now where standing on your principles is causing you pain in other areas; you will have to do some adjustments or a little tweaking — so to speak.

Three kids later and turning twenty-eight, I had my light bulb moment. I started to re-adjust my value and my belief systems holistically. I filed for a divorce. Stopped sacrificing myself for what I thought was right. It turned out to be one of the best decisions of my life. I knew that if my children were to have any kind of decent life, then I had to make a stand.

Developing principles and discovering what you stand on, can be a bit challenging. I'm not saying jump up and change your beliefs because of something or someone else. I will always be open to readjustment because you can be so stuck on something being one way so much that you miss your blessing. You can miss what God has for you because it is not in the package you wanted it in. There will be seasons when you're going to have to fight day and night for what you want in life. Sometimes you may be warranted to dive head first, coming up for some air, then going right back into it to fight again.

Standing on principles, having integrity, a willingness to change, passion, and love, etc. all of these things will give you drive and strength from nowhere. All of a sudden, the heavens will open up and blessings will begin to pour down on you. Stand up for your principles, don't allow something or someone to knock you off your course.

Staying strong and true to who and what you are will ease your walk through the right path. Ensure you do not compromise your dignity and the woman or man that God has called you to be. Recognize what is happening. First of all, you are shaping your family, teaching them that you can be whatever you put your mind to. Don't allow limitations to hinder you and push forward in pursuit of happiness. In the end, these will all become the strength on which you can stand on.

I recall the time I stopped smoking cigarettes —having started since I was thirteen years old. I was 37 at the time, my son had just been diagnosed with asthma. My mom told me, "Erica if it's in your car, your clothes, even if you're not around him when you smoke it will affect him." That was all the inspiration I needed. I woke up the next day and threw out every single stick I could find. I cleaned the house and my car and never looked back.

## Quitting marijuana and drinking, however, did not come to me so easily.

I would often rationalize the behavior by telling myself that it wasn't an everyday thing and I could do it casually. Eventually, at age 41, I finally stopped drinking, and smoking Marijuana.

It was tough because I came from a family who loved to throw a good party with booze aplenty. I would steal the alcohol when the adults were not looking. The alcohol often helped me to block out certain pains and struggles I was going through. Knowing how to deal with them was not my strongest suit at the time. I went on to be an on and off again party girl for over twenty-nine years, causing damage to my reality. Through alcohol, cigarettes, and marijuana, I was able to hide from the light. I was able to hide my true feelings from my neighbor's continued violation of me. I was able to hide getting beat up a lot in school because of my skin color. I was able to hide that fact that it took alcohol for me to be intimate with someone because I was able to go back into a place in my mind that does not cause me to think or feel just do, just be there in the physical. And most damagingly, I was able to hide the fact that God had called me a long time ago to walk in alignment with him. All of these were to my detriment and had an adverse effect on me.

Thinking back, my father and I spent the next three years after our reunification pouring love into each other, laughing and having a great time. Having family picnics in his backyard, Christmas dinners etc. I purchased a "Lazy-Boy" just so he could come over and spend the night whenever he wanted. That was the true moment my life began changing. It was the moment that the missing pieces of the puzzle I had been missing began to fall in place. For the next three years, before his death on October 31, 2017, my father gave me the love that I'd sought for so long, the love I'd looked in all the wrong places to get. That love made me realize that I am worth loving. That I am worth fighting for. It reinforced and assured me that I am powerful. It showed me how I should be treated, my strengths, and what God has called me to do.

## *My life began to change.*

Not too long after that, God brought Pastor Leon McDonald III from The Winners Circle Church. A young gifted pastor who was able to understand and meet me where I was. He began to show me a different kind of love, one different from my father's. His kind of love was the first I had from a man who did not want anything in return from me. He showed me how to have a relationship with God, which in turn helped me open my eyes and discover who I am. The path was not done yet, God sent one more man into my life, and that was my mentor.

Now, I have the power of 4: God, my father, my pastor, and my mentor. My mentor was powerful, his anointing was nothing like I have ever seen before. After a period when he would simply call from time to time to check on me and our paths crossed again, he saw that I was heading down the wrong road without the possibility of recovery. Depression had hit me so hard, I thought this was surely it. But God had other plans for me. He used my mentor to show me things I had never seen before. He showed me that a man can genuinely have an interest in my well-being without attachments.

Through him, God began to breathe life back into me and I began to open up and receive. I applied for a promotion at my day job, it was a team lead position. My mentor started building my confidence and helped me go over the interview process repeatedly. My boss, Laura, had moved my cubicle to the front of the room, to be grouped with the team I bill certain insurances with. I remember fussing, and being really annoyed that she'd moved my seat. I knew that when the owner came up to our floor, I would not be able to hide in the shadows anymore or stay under the radar.

My mentor and I practiced my interview skills, he gave me answers to similar questions he would ask his employees while going through their interview process. I pulled out all the stops and knew for sure that I would be getting the job. I had gone back to college at thirty-five and received my associate degree in Healthcare Administration. Then I attended a program and received my certification in medical billing and coding. I knew no one else in my department was certified or had a degree such as myself. I was ready and excited about life again. After going through the interview process, my boss called me into her office, I was dressed professionally. When she told me that I did not get the job, instead of being downhearted, I was so happy.

## *I was excited about life because I knew God had already started working on me.*

That interview was just the jump start to prepare me for what was to come. I started to hear God speak things to me I had never heard before. I started seeing things I never saw before. The next day, I woke up, and with much happiness, I said, "I am ready," while talking to my mentor on the phone. He responds, "What do you want to do?" I told him, "I want to be a motivational speaker, a coach, I want to do a podcast and write a book." His response was priceless and it was what pushed me into walking in alignment with God's assignment for me. He said, "don't just talk about it, be about it." After that day, I went on to register my business and walk into purpose.

I gained love and friendships like never before. When God has an assignment on your life, a calling to do his will, he will send his people to do his work for him. In order to get to where I am today, to be the woman I was called to be, I had to do the work and be receptive to what God had sent my way. I had to discover who Erica Lynn is and who I wanted to become. Understand the journey and the path you are to travel. You must develop the ability to recognize what your needs are in order to get you there.

# CHAPTER 6

## NEED

There are people, who do not eat on a regular or timely schedule, so their bodies begin to crash, in need of some type of sugar, to keep their engine running. When you pop a piece of candy in their mouth or give them orange juice, their body miraculously rejuvenates. Just like having the realization of who you were, who are you, and who you want to become, coming to an understanding of your needs, and the actualization of your journey on how you have arrived is important.

Pop a dose of life's orange juice and rejuvenate. In order to understand what your needs are, let's take a look back over what has taken place through the road you have traveled so far. Go back through the previous 5 chapters and from each chapter briefly think about what your personal "ah-ha" moment was. What was the one thing from your life that stood out as you read that chapter?

If you have done this, figuring out what you need is relative. When we talked about healing, we understood that in order to heal from abuse, you must first verbalize it i.e. you must first speak about it. I must issue a disclaimer here that I am not a psychologist nor a licensed therapist. Therefore, I always recommend getting professional help if you cannot do it alone or with the self-help tools. I also believe that small group sessions help as well. I have learned that if you speak on a thing and get it out, you release the power that it holds over you. I had an opportunity to speak about the abuse and promiscuousness that took place in my life. Some of my issues, I was able to fix after seeking help, and speaking with my father before he passed. However, the most important thing that I was unable to fix was myself.

## God had to send someone who opened my eyes and showed me that I'd been playing the victim.

I'd played the victim for so long that it got in the way of my healing process. Being able to say it out of my mouth no longer brought life to it. Why is that so Important? Because everybody goes through life with different experiences, and if you listened to someone else's story, you would say 'thank God I did not have to go through what they have gone through.' What I am saying is, we all have challenges in life and what we do with those challenges will shape us. However, what we cannot do is let it define who we are. As I was writing this book, I discovered more things about Erica Lynn and they will be shared throughout the road God continues to send me on. In the journey of taking "1 Step Beyond U", I knew that I had to work harder than I've ever had to work. I had to heal just like every one of you will have to heal.

The concept of chapter two in its entirety is powerful because you cannot do what you need to do if you do not possess the requisite education. Some of you need to go back to school, some need to get mentors, coaches, counselors, or listen to audios on how to heal. While others simply need to read self-help books.

The important thing is that you become educated and obtain the knowledge you need, to understand how to move on to the next episode in your journey. What did I do? I retained several coaches, my mentor, my pastor, my mother, my sisters, my brother, my best friend, and my father. I can never be that person who said no one helped me, that would be a lie. God had a bigger vision for me. In order to see his vision, he knew that it would take all of those people pouring into me. And now, I can give back by pouring into you all.

By the time I reached chapter three, Taking Action,

chapter, I was fired up and raring to go. I was ready to take action. I opened my business and decided on the name, "1 Step Beyond U, LLC." I started speaking it into existence and all the pieces began to fall into place. I said I am ready to help people which required me to give myself to the lord. My prayer was, "Lord, use me as you see fit."

**I gave up the things that were holding me in a crutch: drinking, smoking marijuana, and most importantly, I stopped lying to myself.**

These would appear to be three powerful things to give up for me. I stopped drinking because I did not like the party girl I was when I drank, the flirt that came out in me. To achieve my goal of having business relationships with men and women and earning respect, I had to give up drinking. I gave up marijuana for several reasons. I'd returned to school and in order to retain what I was learning, it was important for me not to cloud up my brain with the effects of marijuana.

It would often make me forgetful or walk around dazed. The biggest reason for quitting smoking, however, was that I had to lead by example. I was walking through the journey with a family member to help them stop smoking and when thirty days passed I said, "wow it has been thirty days, let me start looking for a new job." Although, I did not get a new job or fully pursue it, what I did receive was something much more powerful. My mind began to open up, my brain began retaining information like never before. I started walking around saying, "I can see things I've never seen before; I can hear things I've never heard before."

I know you are saying how is that possible? Well it is possible; do you remember Charlie Brown? When his teacher would talk and all he heard was "wonk wonk wonk". Well, that was all I heard whenever people talked to me. I never retained anything, it would go in one ear and right out through the other. I started living a new life — smoke-free and clear brained. I stopped lying to myself, I stopped telling myself that all I can do is be an employee. That all I am is a product of my past. I stopped being helpless and started being helpful. I stopped being a woman of the streets in my mind and became a woman of GOD.

You too can take action. Stand fast in your journey, do not give up when it seems hard and your past starts to replay itself. When your past rears its head at you, speak on it, do not give it life. Although you acknowledge it, you no longer have to live in it. I want you to appreciate the journey that was set before you. It is time to forgive yourself. It is time to start that business you wanted to start. It is time to be the wonderful mother God has created you to be. It is time to be the best father you can be. It is time to be the best wife or husband you can be.

**_Whatever your desire is, it is time to treat yourself and not cheat yourself. It is time to take action and walk into your purpose._**

You must not look back any further or wear it as a crutch; instead, wear it as a badge of honor in the knowledge that you are strong and have done a lot of work. Take that leap, receive inspiration, and understand your needs. In the words of rapper, Jay Z, "Gon' dust your shoulders off", and move. Move into that level of growth that when someone sees you they say, "something is different about you, I just can't put my finger on it."

# CHAPTER 7

# GROWTH

I have grown so much in my life; the evolution has been mind-blowing. I look back on the journey as the gateway to living my best life. I remember taking drives through some of the richest neighborhoods and envisioning myself in those houses. Walking through the front door into the foyer looking up at the curved staircase, looking at my children as they greet, "hello mom." The feeling I received knowing I put all my efforts toward providing the best life I could for my family.

Then my thoughts would shift to wondering how those people made their money. They must be some type of superstar. The saying goes, "when you know better, you will do better." I learned that these are everyday people just like you and I. They went after the knowledge required to obtain their dream. I no longer look at wealth, big houses, and fancy cars and think, how did they obtain it? I look at it as, how many books do I need to sell? How many seminars and conferences do I need to speak at? What is it that I must do to get this?

I will never forget the feeling that came over me when my daughter was in a scooter accident in Taiwan. The accident sent her body into shock and all the things her body was normally strong enough to fight off before, became too powerful for her. She ended up in the hospital a couple of days before Christmas. An infection had set in and the hospital could not figure out what the cause of the infection was. She ran a fever at 104 degrees for several days.

**I remember feeling so helpless. I remember feeling the guilt for being a selfish mom.**

Selfish by not following my dreams and having enough money in the bank to just jump on a plane to go be with her. I remember not having anyone at the hospital who spoke English. She and I had been on FaceTime so, I could at least see what was going on. I remember praying, "Lord please help my daughter, please protect her and heal her." My son wasn't in Taiwan yet, during this period. I was at one of my lowest points of my life in a long time. In disbelief, I said, "Why can't I be there for my child?"

After three weeks of her being in the hospital, my church, family, friends, and I were all praying for her recovery. One day, I asked her to ask if the doctor in the room could speak English. "Yes I do." came the response. The doctor got on the phone and we started talking and I made a request, "please release her from the hospital. There is a plane waiting for her in three days to bring her back to America. If you release her, I will get all the medical care needed back in America." The doctor said, "I will talk to the resident doctor and I will get back to you,"

The next day, the heavens opened up because they released her the day before her flight was due —with one condition: that I contact the airline and have her put on medical alert and they will have to put her on and take her off the plane in a wheelchair. She was released from the hospital, went home and slept. Then, she took an Uber to her school and wrote her final exam. She had that one professor, who would not allow her to take it, while she was in the hospital.

I remember letting her sleep, then waking her at 6pm Taiwanese time saying, "get up pack your suitcase." I watched her struggle to even muscle up enough strength to lift her arms. She could barely stand. Her roommate would bring her soup and hot tea and make sure she took her medicine.

At 6:00 AM her ride was waiting for her outside. I

watched her on FaceTime as she pulled her suitcase down each step (there was no elevator and she lived on the sixth floor). We were on FaceTime every chance we could, she had gone through Hong Kong and a couple of other places with the airline staff caring for her and God protecting and watching over her. When she arrived, my mom, host son from China and myself were at the airport waiting for her.

**_I will never forget the feeling that I felt once she was in my arms and home again._**

Of course, I immediately took her to the doctor the next day to find out if she had a virus or an infection. The doctor said, "It had to run its course." For six weeks I gave her green smoothies, fixed her three meals a day and made sure she slept as much as possible. At the end of the six weeks, she was all better and ready to go back to college.

I shared this story with you all because that is my why. Why do I exist? Why do I work so hard? Why is it my life's purpose to help others? Why did I become a better person? Why do I have to show my children how to live their best life? My last assignment for you all is to write down your WHY. Ask yourself, "why is growth so important?" "Who am I doing this for and why?" "What is/are the thing(s) that means the most to me?"

# MY WHY

Now when you start on your path of growth and you begin to get weak, or have all of these questions, I want you to think about your why. I want you to visualize it, tune in to it. Speak to it, if you have to. Do not go back to where you came from; instead, go into who you are about to become. When you go, go with your head held high, and your journey alongside of you, ready to share if needed to help someone else.

## Whenever I look back to my growth, I always shed tears of joy.

My children are happy and healthy. My oldest son who was twenty-three at the time, gave up his job at Chrysler to move to Taiwan. His move was not only to be there for my daughter, his sister, but to follow his dream of being a famous producer and artist as well. They have both opened a successful business called, *Formosa Mousa*, which means Taiwan music. All this because they have seen their mom grow from being a woman who was on public assistance until the age of thirty-five into a woman who started a company that is meant to change lives all over the world.

The reason I wrote this book was not to only help you with your healing but also document my continuous journey. With my why, a portion of the sales from this book will be going toward my travels to see my children. The remaining portion will be used to bless deserving families for Christmas, as well as give back to those who have poured into the vision.

My why is my youngest son who God told me to stop sending away because he was a little lost. I sent him to live with his father hoping that he would get what he needed. However, due to his father's health condition, he was unable to meet his needs. God then sent him back home, it was up to me to help him discover himself and what he wanted to become.

This wasn't something I could do alone. So, I enlisted help from my pastor, respected members of my church, and my mentor stepped in and showed me how to help him become a young man. He showed me how to provide him with the tools that gave him room to grow. I realized for the first time, during a conversation with him one night, that had I not poured into him, loved him and met him at that point of his life, he would have ended up having a similar issue to the one I had growing up: the "daddy syndrome" and his would have probably been called the "momma syndrome". That was when it really hit me for the first time. That was when I decided for the first time to spread my wings and knew I must look at things from both sides of the fence and not just my side.

**_Now that you all have gone through the process of healing, it is time for you to move like the wind — refuse to take NO for an answer._**

It is time for you to grow. You have to let go. You have to grow like an eagle, spread your wings and fly. You have to soar into what God has for you. Do not be afraid for he is with you. Become the best version of you that you can be. Grow into your purpose. When you look back, may it only to be a reminder of where you have come from and how much growth you have experienced. Please be purposeful and be full of life. I will ask of you what my mentor asked of me, "**please reach back and help someone else**". I look forward to all your amazing stories of growth.

God bless you.

# ABOUT THE AUTHOR

Born, Erica Gillis, she now goes by the name of Erica Lynn. She is a motivational speaker, coach, podcast host, and author. Erica Lynn is a single mother of three. She owns "1 Step Beyond U, LLC." Established in 2018, her company is designed to help people understand and realize that limitations are only temporary; that, as a person, if you take "1 step beyond U", God will surely do the rest. Erica appreciates the role different people have come to play in her life and as such desires nothing more than to give back to everyone out there in need of help. She hopes to do her best bit and help people become and attain their divine purpose and become the best version of themselves.

You can find her on www.1stepbeyondu.com where you can gain access to her coaching programs, podcast, and all of her future speaking engagements. Always remember, it only takes 1 Step Beyond U.

Made in the USA
Monee, IL
19 March 2020